FLOWERS FOR ALGERNON

Daniel Keyes

EDITORIAL DIRECTOR Justin Kestler
EXECUTIVE EDITOR Ben Florman
DIRECTOR OF TECHNOLOGY Tammy Hepps

SERIES EDITORS John Crowther, Justin Kestler
MANAGING EDITOR Vince Janoski

WRITER Andrew Bujalski
EDITORS Boomie Aglietti, Dennis Quinio

Please submit all comments and questions or report errors to www.sparknotes.com/errors

Printed and bound in the United States

ISBN 1-58663-514-X

INTRODUCTION: STOPPING TO BUY SPARKNOTES ON A SNOWY EVENING

Whose words these are you *think* you know.
Your paper's due tomorrow, though;
We're glad to see you stopping here
To get some help before you go.

Lost your course? You'll find it here.
Face tests and essays without fear.
Between the words, good grades at stake:
Get great results throughout the year.

Once school bells caused your heart to quake
As teachers circled each mistake.
Use SparkNotes and no longer weep,
Ace every single test you take.

Yes, books are lovely, dark, and deep,
But only what you grasp you keep,
With hours to go before you sleep,
With hours to go before you sleep.

CONTENTS

NOTE: This SparkNote refers to the Bantam paperback edition of *Flowers for Algernon*. The work was originally published in short-story form in 1959 and then expanded by the author, Daniel Keyes, into novel form in 1966.

CONTEXT

DANIEL KEYES WAS BORN in 1927 in Brooklyn, New York. After working as a merchant seaman, he attended Brooklyn College, where he earned both bachelor's and master's degrees. He went on to become a fiction editor at Marvel Science Fiction and also worked as a high school teacher for developmentally disabled adults. Having periodically published science-fiction stories since the early 1950s, Keyes drew on his experience in the classroom and his love of science fiction to compose a short story called "Flowers for Algernon" in 1959.

The story, about a mentally retarded man whose IQ is tripled as the result of an experimental operation, was widely acclaimed and enormously popular. The story received one of science fiction's highest honors, the Hugo Award, for best story of the year in 1959. In 1961, a successful television adaptation, *The Two Worlds of Charlie Gordon,* starred Cliff Robertson as Charlie. Still interested in the character of Charlie and the ideas contained in the short story, Keyes set out to enlarge "Flowers for Algernon" into a full-length novel. The result, published in 1966, won the Nebula Award— science fiction's other highest honor—for best novel of the year and expanded dramatically on the popularity of the short story. In 1968, the novel version was adapted again, this time for a feature film called *Charly.* Cliff Robertson reprised his role as Charlie Gordon and won an Academy Award for his performance. The story has since been adapted many times in many media, notably in 1978 as a short-lived Broadway musical, *Charlie and Algernon,* and as a television drama in 2000 starring Matthew Modine.

The novel version of *Flowers for Algernon* was the high point of Daniel Keyes's career, and it remains by far his most popular and most acclaimed work, having been consistently in print for nearly forty years. Keyes has not been a prolific author; since his success with *Flowers for Algernon,* he has written only three more novels and three works of journalism exploring true crime cases. Like *Flowers for Algernon,* both his fiction and nonfiction are primarily focused on the extraordinary complexities of the human mind. One book of journalism, *The Minds of Billy Milligan,* tells the true story of a convicted murderer with multiple personality disorder who claimed to embody twenty-four different personae. In 2000, Keyes published a book called *Algernon, Charlie, and I: A Writer's Journey*, chronicling his relationship with his most famous story, from his first inspiration to write it to his reflections on its continuing success decades later.

The widespread and enduring interest in *Flowers for Algernon* is a testament to the depth and originality of its premise. Many people wonder how their lives would be affected by becoming more, or less, intelligent, and Keyes gives us a glimpse into what such a journey might be like. Though Keyes's background is in science fiction and the novel undoubtedly belongs to that genre, it also transcends the limitations of the genre. Whereas many science-fiction writers alienate mainstream readers by focusing on technology and the inhuman aspects of the worlds they create, Keyes uses science fiction as a springboard for an exploration of universal human themes such as the nature of intellect, the nature of emotion, and how the two interact.

Though *Flowers for Algernon* depends on science fiction to drive its plot—no intelligence-enhancing surgery has yet been attempted or realized—its characters and situations are quite ordinary. The characters are New York City scientists, teachers, bakers, and barbers, not the space rangers and galactic swashbucklers often associated with science fiction. Indeed, Keyes utilizes science fiction's potential for philosophical inquiry and its capacity to explore the extremes of human nature by imagining an altered version of the world. However, he combines these aspects of science fiction with realistic characters in a realistic environment, creating a work that has enthralled both people who are indifferent to science fiction and avid fans of the genre.

PLOT OVERVIEW

CHARLIE GORDON, a mentally retarded thirty-two-year-old man, is chosen by a team of scientists to undergo an experimental surgery designed to boost his intelligence. Alice Kinnian, Charlie's teacher at the Beekman College Center for Retarded Adults, has recommended Charlie for the experiment because of his exceptional eagerness to learn. The directors of the experiment, Dr. Strauss and Professor Nemur, ask Charlie to keep a journal. The entire narrative of *Flowers for Algernon* is composed of the "progress reports" that Charlie writes.

Charlie works at Donner's Bakery in New York City as a janitor and delivery boy. The other employees often taunt him and pick on him, but Charlie is unable to understand that he is the subject of mockery. He believes that his coworkers are good friends. After a battery of tests—including a maze-solving competition with a mouse named Algernon, who has already had the experimental surgery performed on him—Charlie undergoes the operation. He is initially disappointed that there is no immediate change in his intellect, but with work and help from Alice, he gradually improves his spelling and grammar. Charlie begins to read adult books, slowly at first, then voraciously, filling his brain with knowledge from many academic fields. He shocks the workers at the bakery by inventing a process designed to improve productivity. Charlie also begins to recover lost memories of his childhood, most of which involve his mother, Rose, who resented and often brutally punished Charlie for not being normal like other children.

As Charlie becomes more intelligent, he realizes that he is deeply attracted to Alice. She insists on keeping their relationship professional, but it is obvious that she shares Charlie's attraction. When Charlie discovers that one of the bakery employees is stealing from Mr. Donner, he is uncertain what to do until Alice tells him to trust his heart. Delighted by the realization that he is capable of solving moral dilemmas on his own, Charlie confronts the worker and forces him to stop cheating Donner. Not long afterward, Charlie is let go from the bakery because the other workers are disturbed by the sudden change in him, and because Donner can see that Charlie no longer needs his charity. Charlie grows closer to Alice, though whenever the mood becomes too intimate, he experiences a sensation of panic and feels as if his old disabled self is watching him. Charlie recovers memories of his mother beating him for the slightest sexual impulses, and he realizes that this past trauma is likely responsible for his inability to make love to Alice.

Dr. Strauss and Professor Nemur take Charlie and Algernon to a scientific convention in Chicago, where they are the star exhibits. Charlie has become frustrated by Nemur's refusal to recognize his humanity. He feels that Nemur treats him like just another lab animal, even though it is disturbingly clear that Charlie's scientific knowledge has advanced beyond Nemur's. Charlie wreaks havoc at the convention by freeing Algernon from his cage while they are onstage. Charlie flees back to New York with Algernon and gets his own apartment, where the scientists cannot find him. He realizes that Nemur's hypothesis contains an error and that there is a possibility that his intelligence gain will only be temporary.

Charlie meets his neighbor, an attractive, free-spirited artist named Fay Lillman. Charlie does not tell Fay about his past, and he is able to consummate a sexual relationship with her. The foundation that has funded the experiment gives Charlie dispensation to do his own research, so he returns to the lab. However, his commitment to his work begins to consume him, and he drifts away from Fay.

Algernon's intelligence begins to slip, and his behavior becomes erratic. Charlie worries that whatever happens to Algernon will soon happen to him as well. Algernon eventually dies. Fearing a regression to his previous level of intelligence, Charlie visits his mother and sister in order to try to come to terms with his past. He finds the experience moving, thrilling, and devastating. Charlie's mother, now a demented old woman, expresses pride in his accomplishments, and his sister is overjoyed to see him. However, Rose suddenly slips into a delusional flashback and attacks Charlie with a butcher knife. He leaves sobbing, but he feels that he has finally overcome his painful background and become a fully developed individual.

Charlie succeeds in finding the error in Nemur's hypothesis, scientifically proving that a flaw in the operation will cause his intelligence to vanish as quickly as it has come. Charlie calls this phenomenon the "Algernon-Gordon Effect." As he passes through a stage of average intelligence on his way back to retardation, Charlie enjoys a brief, passionate relationship with Alice, but he sends her away as he senses the return of his old self. When Charlie's regression is complete, he briefly returns to his old job at the bakery, where his coworkers welcome him back with kindness.

Charlie forgets that he is no longer enrolled in Alice's night-school class for retarded adults, and he upsets her by showing up. In fact, Charlie has forgotten their entire romantic relationship. Having decided to remove himself from the people who have known him and now feel sorry for him, he checks himself into a home for disabled adults. His last request is for the reader of his manuscript to leave fresh flowers on Algernon's grave.

CHARACTER LIST

Charlie Gordon The protagonist and author of the progress reports that form the text of *Flowers for Algernon*. Charlie is a thirty-two-year-old mentally retarded man who lives in New York City. He works at Donner's Bakery as a janitor and delivery boy. Charlie's friendliness and eagerness to please, along with his childhood feelings of inadequacy, make him the hardest-working student in Alice Kinnian's literacy class for retarded adults. When Charlie undergoes an experimental surgery to increase his intelligence, his IQ skyrockets to the level of a genius. His obsession with untangling his own emotional life and his longing to reach an emotional maturity and inner peace to match his intellectual authority inform many of the novel's primary concerns.

Alice Kinnian Charlie's teacher at the Beekman College Center for Retarded Adults. Alice originally recommends Charlie for the experimental operation because she is impressed by his motivation. Although she is not one of the scientists who perform the experiment on Charlie, she acts as an unofficial member of the team because of her concern for him. She is interested in intellectual pursuits but is ultimately more motivated by emotion. Alice is the one woman with whom Charlie briefly finds loving fulfillment.

Professor Harold Nemur The scientist in charge of the experiment that heightens Charlie's intelligence. An arrogant and career-obsessed man, Nemur treats Charlie as a laboratory animal rather than a human being. Nemur has a tendency to imply that he *created* Charlie, as if his mentally challenged patient is not a human. Nemur is tormented somewhat by his wife, who seems even more fixated on his career than he is.

Dr. Strauss The neurologist and psychiatrist who performs the experimental operation that raises Charlie's intelligence, and Nemur's partner in the experiment. Dr. Strauss conducts therapy sessions with Charlie after the operation. Unlike Nemur, Dr. Strauss maintains interest in and concern for Charlie's emotional development.

Burt Selden A friendly graduate student who is working on his thesis and who assists Strauss and Nemur in conducting the experiment. Burt oversees the testing of both Charlie and Algernon. He introduces Charlie to some of the students and faculty at Beekman College.

Algernon The white mouse that is the first successful test subject for the experimental operation Charlie later undergoes. The operation makes Algernon three times as intelligent as a normal mouse and enables him to solve complex puzzles.

Fay Lillman Charlie's neighbor in the apartment building that he moves into after running away from the scientific convention. Fay is an attractive, free-spirited, and sexually liberal artist whose favorite pastimes are drinking and dancing. She embarks on a brief affair with Charlie, knowing nothing about his background.

Rose Gordon Charlie's mother, a domineering woman terribly ashamed of Charlie's retardation. In the early part of his childhood, Rose refused to accept that Charlie was abnormal, despite her husband's appeals for her to be rational. Rose finally had another child, Norma, on whom she focused all of her energy. Rose routinely punished Charlie for any sign of sexual interest, as she could not accept the notion of her retarded son having any form of sexuality.

Matt Gordon Charlie's father, a barbershop-supply salesman who always wanted to open his own barbershop, and eventually does. Although Matt tried to protect the young Charlie from Rose's hostility, he gave in too easily to her bullying.

Norma Gordon Charlie's younger sister, who grows up to act as caretaker for their mentally unstable mother. During their childhood, Norma resented Charlie for getting what she perceived as special treatment and was cruel to him. When she reencounters Charlie as an adult, however, she is glad to see him and regrets her youthful spite.

Uncle Herman Charlie's uncle, who took care of Charlie after Rose expelled him from her home. Herman was generous to Charlie, protected him from neighborhood bullies, and set him up with his longtime job at Donner's Bakery. At the beginning of the novel, Herman has been dead for years.

Mr. Donner The owner of the bakery where Charlie works. A friend of Uncle Herman, Mr. Donner agreed to hire Charlie so he would not have to go to the Warren State Home upon Herman's death. Donner gave Herman his word that he would look out for Charlie's interests. Donner stands by his pledge faithfully and treats Charlie like family.

Frank Reilly and Joe Carp Two employees at Donner's Bakery who often pick on Charlie. Frank and Joe play tricks on Charlie and make him the butt of jokes that he does not understand. However, Frank and Joe think of themselves as Charlie's friends and defend him when others pick on him.

Gimpy A baker at Donner's Bakery who secretly steals from his boss. Gimpy got his nickname because of his limp. His relationship with Charlie is much like Frank and Joe's relationship with Charlie.

Fanny Birden The only bakery employee who is consistently nice to Charlie. Fanny does not like to see the others pick on Charlie because of his disability. When Charlie becomes a genius, Fanny is glad for him but is highly suspicious and wonders if he has made a deal with the devil.

Dr. Guarino A quack doctor to whom Charlie was taken as a child. Dr. Guarino promised Rose that he could scientifically increase Charlie's intelligence, but his methods are a complete sham. Guarino, however, was kind to Charlie.

Hilda　　The nurse on duty while Charlie is first recovering from his operation. Hilda believes that Charlie may be defying God's will by trying to gain intelligence unnaturally.

Minnie　　An ordinary female mouse Fay purchases so that Algernon can have a companion.

Meyer Klaus A brutish new employee at Donner's Bakery who is working there when Charlie briefly reassumes his job after losing his temporary intelligence.

CHARACTER LIST

Analysis of Major Characters

Charlie Gordon

Charlie is the narrator and the main character of the novel, and his miraculous transformation from mental disability to genius sets the stage for Keyes to address a number of broad themes and issues. Charlie's lack of intelligence has made him a trusting and friendly man, as he assumes that the people in his life—most notably, his coworkers at Donner's Bakery—are as well intentioned as he is. As his intelligence grows, however, Charlie gains perspective on his past and present. He realizes that people have often taken advantage of him and have been cruel to him for sport, knowing that he would not understand. Likewise, he realizes that when people have been kind to him, it usually has been out of condescension or out of an awareness that he is inferior. These realizations cause Charlie to grow suspicious of nearly everyone around him. Interestingly, the experimental operation elevates Charlie's intelligence to such an extent that his new genius distances him from people as much as his disability does. Charlie eventually convinces himself that he has lost feeling even for Alice Kinnian, the one person whom he feels has never betrayed him and the only one for whom he has maintained a deep affection throughout his life.

Feeling isolated from humanity, Charlie pursues a course of self-education and struggles to untangle his emotional life. He comes to feel that his mind contains two people: the new, genius Charlie, who wants to reach emotional maturity, and the older, disabled Charlie, whose actions are largely informed by the fear and shame his mother, Rose, instilled in him. To reach his goal, the new Charlie must come to grips with the traumas the old Charlie experienced.

Although Charlie resents the mistreatment he endured while disabled, he harbors hostility toward his old self and, ironically, feels the same lack of respect for his intellectual inferiors that many others used to feel for him. It is only in the final weeks of Charlie's heightened intelligence, before he reverts to his previous mental retardation, that he learns to forgive his family and give and receive love. Charlie's brief moment of emotional grace comes in the form of the fulfilling but fleeting romantic affair he has with Alice. Finally, though Charlie lapses back to his original state at the end of the novel, a newfound sense of self-worth remains within him, despite the fact that he has lost his short-lived intelligence.

ALICE KINNIAN

Alice Kinnian is the one person with whom Charlie comes to experience a truly fulfilling personal relationship. It is fitting that throughout the novel Alice represents the human warmth and kindness that persist in the face of the intellectual and scientific focus of many of the other characters. Alice teaches literacy skills to mentally retarded adults because she cares about and enjoys working with her students; she does not believe that their disabilities make them lesser human beings. She takes genuine satisfaction in helping people and recommends Charlie for Nemur and Strauss's experiment because she admires Charlie's desire to learn. Charlie appreciates Alice's concern for his well-being; she is a constant presence in his earliest progress reports, even though she is not a member of the scientific team that is examining him.

In Alice's concern and affection lie the seeds of her eventual romantic love for Charlie. Though she is often deeply confused throughout their relationship, uncertain of what is and is not appropriate in their unique situation, Alice displays unwavering care for Charlie as his IQ boomerangs up and back down again. Her ability to accept Charlie as a person of any level of intelligence sets Alice apart from the other characters in the novel, who consistently judge Charlie only on his intellect. Though she is driven by emotion, Alice is not at all anti-intellectual; on the contrary, she is fascinated by academia and high culture. Though intellect and emotion seem to be opposed throughout the novel, Alice's intellectual leanings demonstrate that one need not sacrifice his or her ability to love in order to enjoy a life of the mind.

PROFESSOR NEMUR

If Alice represents the possibility of an emotionally healthy adulthood, Nemur represents the opposite. He is a man of great intellect but little ability to relate to others. Unlike his partner, Dr. Strauss, Nemur is never interested in Charlie's human emotions; he cares only about Charlie's quantifiable progress as an experimental subject. Professor Nemur thinks of Charlie just as he thinks of Algernon—as a laboratory animal. Pressured by a domineering wife, Nemur is desperate to advance his career and longs for his peers to regard him as brilliant. Nemur cannot stand to be shown up by anyone—not by Strauss, and certainly not by Charlie. He is deeply perturbed when Charlie surpasses him intellectually and takes command of the experiment. Though Charlie resents Nemur for most of the novel, we see after the operation that Charlie himself is potentially at risk of becoming cold and loveless like Nemur.

ROSE GORDON

Obsessed by an imaginary ideal of normalcy, Rose initially responded to Charlie's mental disability with denial. She insisted that her son was normal, and she developed a delusional theory that he was brilliant but was cursed by jealous neighborhood mothers. Her refusal to accept her son's disability was demonstrated by her decision to name Charlie's younger sister Norma because it sounds like "normal." After Norma's birth, Rose turned her full attention to Norma's success and tried to ignore Charlie altogether. Signs of Charlie's progression toward adulthood, especially his manifestations of sexuality, infuriated Rose. She demanded that Charlie be removed from her home. By denying his existence, she also denied what she perceived to be her failure as a mother.

When Charlie, now brilliant after his operation, visits an aged Rose near the end of the novel, her capacity for denial has grown into full-fledged dementia. She switches back and forth from recognizing Charlie to thinking he is a stranger, and back and forth from pride at his recent accomplishments to an irrational fear that he has come back to molest Norma. In her old age, Rose has been driven entirely mad by her overwhelming yet doomed desire to be what she perceives as normal.

THEMES, MOTIFS & SYMBOLS

THEMES

Themes are the fundamental and often universal ideas explored in a literary work.

MISTREATMENT OF THE MENTALLY DISABLED

The fictional idea of artificially augmenting or diminishing intelligence enables Keyes to offer a telling portrayal of society's mistreatment of the mentally disabled. As Charlie grows more intelligent after his operation, effectively transforming from a mentally retarded man to a genius, he realizes that people have always based their attitudes toward him on feelings of superiority. For the most part, other people have treated Charlie not only as an intellectual inferior but also as less of a human being than they are. While some, like his coworkers at the bakery, have treated him with outright cruelty, others have tried to be kind but ultimately have been condescending in their charity.

After his operation, Charlie himself drifts into a condescending and disrespectful attitude toward the disabled to a certain extent. Charlie consciously wants to treat his new intellectual inferiors as he wishes others had treated him. When he sees patrons at a diner laughing at a mentally retarded busboy, he demands that the patrons recognize the boy's humanity. However, when Charlie visits the Warren State Home, he is horrified by the dim faces of the disabled people he meets, and he is unable to muster any warmth toward them. Charlie fears the patients at Warren State because he does not want to accept that he was once like them and may soon be like them again. We may even interpret Charlie's reaction as his own embodiment of the same fear of abnormality that has driven his mother to madness.

Thus, while Keyes condemns the act of mistreating the mentally disabled, he also displays an understanding of why this mistreatment occurs, enabling his readers to see through the eyes of someone who has experienced such ridicule firsthand. Charlie struggles with a tendency toward the same prejudice and condescension he has seen in other people. However, Charlie's dual perspective allows him to understand that he is as human as anyone else, regardless of his level of intelligence.

THE TENSION BETWEEN INTELLECT AND EMOTION

The fact that Charlie's mental retardation affects both his intellectual and emotional development illustrates the difficulty—but not the impossibility—of developing both aspects simultaneously and without conflict. Charlie is initially warmhearted and trusting, but as his intelligence increases he grows cold, arrogant, and disagreeable. The more he understands about the world, the more he recoils from human contact. At his loneliest point, in Progress Report 12, Charlie shockingly decides that his genius has effectively erased his love for Alice.

Professor Nemur and Fay indicate the incompatibility of intellect and emotion. Nemur is brilliant but humorless and friendless. Conversely, Fay acts foolishly and illogically because she is ruled entirely by her feelings. It is only with Alice's encouragement that Charlie finally realizes he does not have to choose between his brain and his heart, the extremes represented by Nemur and Fay. Charlie learns to integrate intellect and emotion, finding emotional pleasure in both his intellectual work and his relationships. It is in this phase that he finds true fulfillment with Alice.

THE PERSISTENCE OF THE PAST IN THE PRESENT

Charlie's recovery of his childhood memories after his operation illustrates how significantly his past is embedded in his understanding of the present. Charlie's past resurfaces at key points in his present experience, taking the form of the old Charlie, whom the new Charlie perceives as a separate entity that exists outside of himself. In a sense, the past, as represented by the old Charlie, literally keeps watch over the present. When Charlie longs to make love to Alice, the old Charlie panics and distracts him—a sign that the shame Rose instilled in Charlie is still powerful, even if he cannot remember the origin of this shame.

Charlie cannot move forward with his emotional life until he understands and deals with the traumas of childhood. Similar ties to the past control Charlie's mother. When Charlie returns to see Rose, she still harbors her old resentment over Charlie's lack of normalcy—even after his intelligence levels have increased dramatically. Rose's attempt to attack Charlie with a knife illustrates that for her, just as for Charlie, the past interferes with her actions and concerns in the present. Rose cannot separate her memories of the retarded Charlie from the genius Charlie who comes to visit her in the flesh. The harrowing turn of events at this meeting is a tragic reminder of the past's pervasive influence on the present.

MOTIFS

Motifs are recurring structures, contrasts, or literary devices that can help to develop and inform the text's major themes.

CHANGES IN GRAMMAR, SPELLING, AND PUNCTUATION
Charlie's initial leaps forward in mental ability are conveyed less by *what* he writes than by *how* he writes. Keyes signals Charlie's changing mental state through the level of accuracy or inaccuracy of the grammar, spelling, and punctuation in Charlie's progress reports. The first sentence of the novel, typical of Charlie's early reports, is rife with errors: "Dr Strauss says I shoud rite down what I think and remembir and evrey thing that happins to me from now on." By Progress Report 9, we see Charlie's immense progress in his composition of flawless sentences: "I had a nightmare last night, and this morning, after I woke up, I free-associated the way Dr. Strauss told me to do when I remember my dreams." Similarly, Keyes initially conveys the loss of Charlie's intelligence at the end with the erosion of his grammar, spelling, and punctuation.

FLASHBACKS
Starting in Progress Report 9, Charlie is overwhelmed by a series of flashbacks to events from his youth. These flashbacks are provoked by experiences in the present: when Charlie is propositioned by the pregnant woman in Central Park, for example, he recalls his mother's pregnancy with his sister. All of Charlie's memories come in the form of such revelations and recall events of which he was not previously aware. These new memories hold new lessons for Charlie about his past and shed new light on his present neuroses. The flashbacks are interspersed with the narrative, so that the stories of Charlie's present and past intertwine and reflect upon each other.

THE SCIENTIFIC METHOD

Charlie and Algernon are subjects in scientific experiments, and as Charlie becomes intelligent, he actually ends up internalizing much of the scientific methodology to which he has been subjected. Not only does Charlie become well versed in the technicalities of science, surpassing Professor Nemur's knowledge, but he also approaches his emotional problems in a scientific manner. When Charlie realizes that the feelings of shame triggered by his emotional attachment to Alice render him incapable of making love to her, he devises a scientific experiment to test this principle. Charlie decides to try to pretend that Alice is Fay, to whom he is not so emotionally attached, in order to see if doing so will allow him to make love without panicking. Charlie is unable to go through with this experiment, however, because he realizes that he would be effectively placing Alice in the dehumanizing role of laboratory animal, a role he finds deplorable. The scientific pursuit of knowledge becomes Charlie's guiding principle, but he is aware of the dangers of dehumanization that accompany it. In the end, when Charlie knows his intelligence will desert him and he contemplates suicide, he decides that he must go on living and continue to keep progress reports so that he can pass on knowledge of his unique journey.

SYMBOLS

Symbols are objects, characters, figures, or colors used to represent abstract ideas or concepts.

ALGERNON

As Algernon and Charlie undergo the same operation and the same testing, Algernon's developments are good predictors of Charlie's future. When Algernon begins to lose his intelligence, it is a chilling indication that Charlie's own mental gains will be short-lived. Algernon also symbolizes Charlie's status as a subject of the scientists: locked in a cage and forced to run through mazes at the scientists' whim, Algernon is allowed no dignity and no individuality. Charlie's freeing of Algernon from his cage and simultaneous decision to abandon the laboratory makes Algernon's physical liberation a symbol of, and a precursor to, his own emotional independence.

Adam and Eve and the Tree of Knowledge

The story of Adam and Eve, mentioned by Hilda, the nurse, and Fanny at the bakery, and then alluded to again in Charlie's reading of John Milton's *Paradise Lost,* bears a symbolic resemblance to Charlie's journey from retardation to genius. Adam and Eve eat the fruit of the tree of knowledge, which costs them their innocence and causes them to be cast out of the Garden of Eden. As the forbidden fruit does for Adam and Eve, Charlie's operation gives him the mental capacity to understand the world that he previously lacks. Just as it does to Adam and Eve, this knowledge causes Charlie to lose his innocence, not only in the form of his sexual virginity, but also in the form of his growing emotional bitterness and coldness. Hilda and Fanny both imply that Charlie, like Adam and Eve, has defied God's will by becoming more intelligent. Charlie's discovery that artificially induced intelligence cannot last implies that God or nature abhors unnatural intelligence. However, Keyes leaves us to judge for ourselves whether Charlie deserves the punishment of mental regression.

The Window

Many of Charlie's childhood memories involve looking through a window, which symbolizes the emotional distance that Charlie feels from others of normal mental ability. Shunned by his peers because of his disability, he remembers watching the other children play through a window in his apartment. When Charlie becomes intelligent, he often feels as if the boyhood Charlie is watching him through windows. The window represents all of the factors that keep the mentally retarded Charlie from feeling connected to society.

Charlie's increased intelligence enables him to cross over to the other side of the window, a place where members of society accept him. However, in crossing over, Charlie becomes just as distant from his former self as the children he used to see playing outside. When Charlie regresses into disability, he maintains an indefinable sense of his former genius self, but he says, "I dont think its me because its like I see him from the window." The window is the unbridgeable divide between the two Charlies. The only point at which the brilliant Charlie feels that he is confronting the other Charlie face-to-face is when he drunkenly sees himself in a mirror, effectively a window to one's interior self.

SYMBOLS

Summary & Analysis

Progress Reports 1–7

NOTE: Flowers for Algernon *is told in the form of "progress reports" kept by Charlie Gordon, a mentally retarded man who is chosen as the subject of a laboratory experiment designed to increase his intelligence.*

SUMMARY: "PROGRIS RIPORT I MARTCH 3"
In his first "progris riport," Charlie has an IQ of sixty-eight and is a poor speller. He is thirty-two years old, has a menial job at Donner's Bakery, and takes Miss Alice Kinnian's literacy class three times a week at the Beekman College Center for Retarded Adults. Dr. Strauss, who along with Professor Nemur is a director of the experiment, has instructed Charlie to write everything he thinks and feels in these progress reports.

SUMMARY: "PROGRIS RIPORT 2 — MARCH 4"
A man named Burt Selden has given Charlie a "raw shok" test. Burt shows Charlie a stack of white cards with ink spilled on them—called a Rorschach inkblot test—and asks Charlie to tell him what he sees in the ink. The literal-minded Charlie, unable to grasp the concept of imagination, says that he sees only spilled ink. He worries that he has "faled" the test.

SUMMARY: "3D PROGRIS RIPORT"
Dr. Strauss and Professor Nemur have tested an intelligence-building procedure on animals and are now looking for a human subject. Alice has recommended Charlie because of the eagerness to learn he has displayed in her literacy class. When Strauss and Nemur question Charlie about this eagerness, Charlie mentions that his mother encouraged his education as a child. The doctors tell Charlie that they need permission from his family to go ahead with the operation, but Charlie is not sure where they live or whether they are still alive. Charlie worries that staying up late to work on reports is making him tired at his bakery job, where a coworker recently yelled at him for dropping a tray of rolls.

SUMMARY: "PROGRIS RIPORT 4"

A woman gives Charlie a test in which she shows him pictures of people he has never seen and asks him to invent stories about them. As with the "raw shok" test, Charlie does not understand the point of making up stories and tells the woman that as a child he would be hit if he lied. Burt then takes Charlie to a psychology laboratory, where he shows Charlie a mouse named Algernon who has already undergone Strauss and Nemur's experimental surgery. Burt has Charlie compete with Algernon by attempting to solve a maze on paper while Algernon runs through an identical maze. Algernon beats Charlie every time.

SUMMARY: "PROGRIS RIPORT 5 MAR 6"

Charlie says that the scientists have located his sister and have received her permission to proceed with the operation. He listens to a conversation between Strauss, Nemur, and Burt. Though Nemur fears that dramatically increasing Charlie's "eye-Q" will make him sick, Strauss argues that Charlie's motivation to learn is a great advantage. Nemur tries to explain to Charlie that the operation is experimental and that they cannot be certain that it will succeed in making Charlie smarter. There is even the potential that the operation will succeed temporarily but ultimately leave Charlie worse off than he is now. Charlie is not worried, however, as he is thrilled to have been chosen and vows to "try awful hard" to become smarter.

SUMMARY: "PROGRIS RIPORT 6th Mar 8"

I just want to be smart like other pepul so I can have lots of frends who like me. (See QUOTATIONS, p. 47)

Charlie is in the hospital awaiting his operation. Alice visits him, and Charlie senses that she is concerned. He is nervous but still excited by the prospect of becoming smarter, and he cannot wait to beat Algernon in a maze race. Charlie also looks forward to being as intelligent as other people so that he can make friends.

SUMMARY: "PROGRESS REPORT 7 MARCH 11"

Three days have passed after the operation, and Charlie does not feel any change. A nurse named Hilda tells him how to spell "progress report," so he diligently begins to correct his misspellings. Hilda also suggests to Charlie that God did not make him smart to begin with and that perhaps Nemur and Strauss should not be tampering with God's will. The next day, Hilda is replaced. When Charlie asks the new nurse how babies are made, she is embarrassed and does not answer. Alice comes to visit. When Charlie expresses disappointment that the operation has not made him smart right away, she reassures Charlie that she has faith in him.

ANALYSIS: PROGRESS REPORTS 1-7

These opening scenes present the main characters and situations of the novel and introduce the novel's unusual narrative form. Charlie's diary-like progress reports gracefully mirror the focus of the story—the rise and fall of his mental abilities. Everything we see is filtered through Charlie's mind, so as his intelligence increases, we see gradual improvements in his vocabulary, grammar, and spelling. In a sense, by peering into his progress reports, we are thrust into the role of doctor, cued to be alert to signs of Charlie's changing mental ability.

Keyes strikes a balance between staying true to Charlie's rough writing style and giving us enough information to understand the situations in which Charlie finds himself, even in instances when Charlie himself does not understand these situations. Though Charlie does not know what a "raw shok" test is, we can surmise from his description that he is being given a Rorschach test. Similarly, when Hilda the nurse disappears the day after she suggests Charlie's operation is sinful, we assume that Nemur and Strauss have removed her, though this idea does not occur to Charlie.

While Charlie's cumbersome language is crude, he includes enough details for us to learn quite a bit about his temperament and background. These details suggest that there is far more to Charlie than initially meets the eye. For instance, he frequently mentions his extraordinary desire to "get smart," a detail that resurfaces when Charlie hears the doctors mention his motivation as the reason he has been chosen for the experiment. Charlie clearly illustrates his motivation through his habit of writing down words he does not know, such as "PSYCHOLOGY LABORATORY" and "THEMATIC APPERCEPTION TEST." Furthermore, Charlie's remarks that his mother encouraged his education as a child but would also hit him for lying begin to hint at the complex nature of Charlie's relationship with Rose. This mother-son relationship provides much of the hidden motivation for Charlie's actions, and the novel explores it in great depth later, as Charlie recovers forgotten memories of his youth.

SUMMARY & ANALYSIS

Nearly all of the novel's major characters are introduced in this opening section, and we can see early on that Charlie's assumptions about these characters are often incomplete or incorrect. When Charlie writes of a bakery coworker, "Gimpy hollers at me all the time when I do something rong, but he reely likes me because hes my frend," we wonder whether Gimpy might be less of a "frend" than Charlie realizes. Most significantly, we meet Alice Kinnian, whose mere presence in these early scenes is a strong indication of her attachment to Charlie. While Strauss and Nemur are present to observe Charlie scientifically, Alice is always there strictly out of concern for his welfare. Because we are seeing everything through Charlie's eyes, which at this point are limited in their perception, the depth and origins of Alice's care for Charlie remain cloudy to us. However, Keyes has Charlie drop hints for us, mentioning that Alice looks "kind of nervus and skared" when she visits just before Charlie's operation. Her apparent anxiety demonstrates that she is worried about the experiment going wrong.

Hilda's comment that Strauss and Nemur are overstepping their moral boundaries alludes to the biblical tale of Adam and Eve, and God's punishment of the couple for eating the forbidden fruit from the tree of knowledge. The sin of Adam is an important metaphor for Charlie's situation in the novel—like Adam, Charlie yearns for knowledge but can only attain it by unnatural means without understanding the consequences. After eating the fruit, Adam and Eve lose their innocence, experience a sexual awakening, and are forced to enter the world outside the Garden of Eden. By drawing a parallel to this story, Keyes foreshadows the fate that awaits Charlie.

PROGRESS REPORTS 8–9

SUMMARY: PROGRESS REPORT 8

Charlie anxiously awaits the effects of the operation, as he is still losing his maze races with Algernon. Charlie eats lunch with Burt in the college cafeteria and overhears the students discussing art, politics, and religion. Charlie does not know what these subjects are, but he longs to understand them. He goes back to work at the bakery, where his coworkers Joe Carp, Gimpy, and Frank Reilly taunt him. Charlie does not understand that he is the butt of their jokes. He writes that his coworkers sometimes refer to "pull[ing] a Charlie Gordon," and Gimpy uses the phrase to describe a new employee's misplacement of a birthday cake. Ever eager to improve himself, Charlie asks Mr. Donner if he can learn to be an apprentice baker, but Donner tells him that he should focus on his cleaning.

Dr. Strauss and Professor Nemur bring Charlie an odd television-like machine that plays images and speaks to him while he sleeps to help him "get smart." Charlie is skeptical; he complains that the machine keeps him awake and makes him tired at work. However, one night the machine triggers a memory, a recollection of the first time Charlie went to Alice's class, determined to learn to read. Charlie begins attending therapy sessions with Dr. Strauss, though he is not sure what purpose they serve. Dr. Strauss explains to Charlie the concept of the conscious and subconscious mind, and says that the television-like device is designed to teach Charlie's subconscious while he sleeps. Dr. Strauss also gives Charlie a dictionary.

After work one day, Frank and Joe take Charlie to a bar, where they urge him to dance like a buffoon and then abandon him. Not comprehending that he is being made fun of, Charlie laughs along. Back at the lab, Charlie finally beats Algernon in a maze race. He also begins to remember more about his family. Charlie recalls one time as a child when his sister, Norma, mocked him for saying he wanted to be a painter. Alice comes to teach Charlie in the laboratory. They begin to read *Robinson Crusoe*, the hardest book Charlie has ever encountered, and together they work on his spelling skills.

Summary: PROGRESS REPORT 9

Charlie shocks everyone in the bakery by proving that he is capable of working the dough mixer, and he gets promoted. He finishes *Robinson Crusoe* and, wanting to know what happens to the characters after the novel ends, becomes frustrated when Alice tells him that the story does not continue beyond the end of the novel. Charlie recovers another memory from his childhood, an episode from Norma's infancy: Charlie had tried to pick Norma up to stop her from crying, but his mother screamed at him and told him never to touch the baby.

Alice begins to teach Charlie about grammar and punctuation. He does not immediately grasp the concepts, but one night something clicks in his mind. In the entry of April 8 it is clear that Charlie has mastered punctuation, literally overnight. Frank and Joe take Charlie out again and make him dance with a girl, but this time

Charlie realizes that they are mocking him, and he suddenly experiences anger and confusion. He dreams about the girl who had danced with him and wakes up with the sheets "wet and messy."

Charlie recovers more memories. He recalls a time when his Uncle Herman protected him from bullies. Charlie also remembers an incident in which a childhood companion nastily rewrote a Valentine's note Charlie had written to a girl at his school, making the girl's brother furious and forcing Charlie to move to a new school.

Charlie's reading, writing, and ability to retain information show sharp daily improvements. He takes another Rorschach test, and he gets angry when he remembers his first "raw shok" experience. Charlie insists that during the first administration of the test Burt told him to find specific secret pictures hidden in the inkblots, not simply to imagine his own pictures. Nemur plays back a tape recording of the first administration of the test, and Charlie is shocked to learn that he is wrong: Burt gave Charlie identical instructions in both sessions, but Charlie lacked the mental capacity to understand them the first time. Charlie is stunned to hear the childishness of his own voice in the tape recording. He decides that he wants to keep some of his progress reports private, though he does not entirely understand why he feels such a need.

ANALYSIS: PROGRESS REPORTS 8–9

Keyes creates great suspense with the operation in Progress Report 8, and we await Charlie's transformation as anxiously as he does. Most of the section is frozen in a holding pattern, as there are few suggestions of increased intelligence and Charlie begins to grow frustrated. This suspense is relieved in Progress Report 9 as Charlie's mental capacities leap to an average or above-average level. His spelling, grammar, and punctuation improve until, in the last entries of the section, his reports read like flawless prose. Similarly, Charlie's new ability to read challenging books like *Robinson Crusoe* demonstrates his greatly increased intellectual capacity.

Charlie's first mental triumph is the relatively minor achievement of operating the dough mixer at the bakery. He has seen this machine in use for seventeen years, but only now is he able to apply his observations so as to attain a true understanding of the machine's operations. We also see that Charlie is now able to grasp abstract concepts, and he suddenly comprehends the concept of the Rorschach test. Furthermore, though it may be the least of his accomplishments intellectually, Charlie's ability to beat Algernon at the maze race is a significant symbolic victory.

While Charlie has clearly developed intellectually, we also see signs of emotional development, which unfortunately are often painful for Charlie. When Alice and Charlie finish *Robinson Crusoe*, Alice tells him that he cannot learn anything more about the characters. Charlie is desperate to know "WHY," and the lack of a satisfying answer to this question greatly distresses him. He is similarly horrified by his sudden realization that his friends from the bakery have been tormenting him for fun. This recognition makes Charlie suspicious of other seemingly friendly people, such as Burt. Charlie's desire to keep his reports private, which he expresses at the end of Progress Report 9, demonstrates that he is beginning to question Nemur and Strauss's objectives as well.

Though Charlie's intellect gives him the ability to challenge his old assumptions and develop a more mature perspective on the world, it also throws him into confusion. He understands that his retardation has caused people to treat him spitefully, and he attempts to reverse this phenomenon. When he first beats Algernon in the maze race, Charlie immediately shifts from resenting the mouse to feeling compassion for him. Charlie's instinct is to treat Algernon, now his mental inferior, as he wishes others had treated him.

Charlie is confused by the novelty of his newfound emotions and by his sudden realization of the complexity of the world around him. He is mystified by the wet dream he has about the woman he dances with at the party. Charlie begins to experience embarrassment, which signals his new awareness of what others think of him. This embarrassment is one of the reasons Charlie suddenly wishes to keep some of his reports private. Additionally, as we see later, much of Charlie's embarrassment stems from events in his childhood that have caused him to associate sexuality with shame. Charlie is sometimes incapable of dealing with his emotional confusion, and this inability occasionally manifests itself as hostility, as we see in the Rorschach test incident.

Charlie's recovery of multiple memories about his childhood is perhaps the most significant component of his personal development, and also contributes to the development of the story as a whole. The history of Charlie's childhood is slowly revealed, and throughout the novel these recollections accompany and influence Charlie's development in the present. His early memories are hazy, but they demonstrate a clear pattern: as a child, Charlie was always under suspicion—even his mother did not trust him to hold his sister—with no one taking his side except Uncle Herman.

Though its settings are mundane and its story is concerned above all with human emotion and interaction, *Flowers for Algernon* is a science-fiction novel in the sense that it uses speculative science and technology as the vehicle for its narrative development. It is a convention of the genre that the science and technology need never be fully explained or convincing. Just as we are asked to suspend our disbelief about the mysterious operation Charlie undergoes, in this section we are introduced to a mysterious television-like machine that helps him learn. Though such a machine may seem unrealistic, Keyes wants the emotional impact of Charlie's story to outweigh any doubts we might have about the practicality of the plot.

PROGRESS REPORTS 10–11

SUMMARY: PROGRESS REPORT 10

Charlie reconfigures the machines at the bakery to increase productivity, which earns him another raise. He remembers a time—referring to himself in the third person not as "I" but as "Charlie"—when Gimpy tried to teach him to make rolls but he was unable to get it right. Charlie notices that his increased intelligence does not make his acquaintances proud of him; instead, they are uncomfortable and upset by his presence. Charlie decides to ask Alice out to a movie to celebrate his raise, though he is unsure if such an invitation is appropriate. Strauss and Nemur agree to let Charlie keep some reports private, and this makes him more comfortable writing about personal matters.

Charlie overhears Nemur and Strauss arguing about whether to present their preliminary findings at an upcoming convention in Chicago. Strauss thinks it is premature, but as the senior member of the research team, Nemur overrides Strauss's objections. Noting the pettiness of the scientists' argument, Charlie realizes that despite their intelligence they are flawed and fallible men.

Charlie befriends some of the college students he meets on campus, and he joyfully discusses Shakespeare with them. They also discuss God, which causes Charlie to comprehend the enormity of religion for the first time. Charlie later has a dream that triggers a flashback of his mother crying out, "He's normal! He's normal!" when he was six years old. He also remembers his father's attempts to force his mother to accept her son's retardation. Charlie remembers his mother hysterically spanking him for defecating in his pants. He finally recalls his parents' names, Matt and Rose.

SUMMARY: PROGRESS REPORT 11
Charlie takes Alice (he now calls her "Alice" rather than "Miss Kinnian") to the movies. He realizes his attraction to her, and their physical proximity flusters him. Charlie confesses his attraction to Alice over dinner. She replies that it would be inappropriate, for the sake of the experiment, for them to develop a romance. Charlie is upset that the books he reads do not offer solutions to the emotional turmoil he is experiencing. He has a childhood memory of discovering Norma's underpants in the laundry hamper, crusted with menstrual blood.

Charlie is distraught to discover that Gimpy has been stealing from the bakery, undercharging customers in exchange for kickbacks. Charlie agonizes over whether he should tell Mr. Donner, and he asks both Nemur and Strauss for advice. Strauss insists that Charlie has a moral obligation to tell, but Nemur argues that he should not become involved. Nemur states that Charlie was practically an "inanimate object" before the operation and thus not accountable. This idea angers Charlie immensely, and he feels that Nemur does not understand that he was a person even in his original disabled condition. Charlie asks Alice for advice about the dilemma, and she tells him that he must feel his own decision from within.

Charlie suddenly understands that he is capable of making moral judgments himself. He decides to confront Gimpy and give him the opportunity to mend his ways before he goes to Donner with his concerns. Trapped, Gimpy grudgingly agrees, clearly disconcerted by Charlie's inexplicable intelligence. Thinking about Alice's role in his newfound independence, Charlie decides that he is in love with her. Meanwhile, Charlie's intellectual pursuits advance far beyond an average level, and he now finds the college professors to be too limited and shortsighted to interest him.

Charlie takes Alice to a concert in Central Park. Shortly after putting his arm around her, he sees a teenage boy watching them, his pants undone. Charlie chases after the boy but cannot find him. Later, he decides that the boy must have been a hallucination, which he thinks arose because his intellectual growth has outpaced his emotional growth. Charlie has a genius's IQ but is emotionally adolescent.

Pressured by his other employees, Donner fires Charlie from the bakery. Charlie is surprised at how much he misses the job, realizing for the first time how much it meant to him. Fanny, a kindly coworker, feels sorry for Charlie, but she also fears his sudden change. Fanny explains to Charlie the story of Adam and Eve and the tree of knowledge. Later, Charlie goes to Alice's apartment. They approach intimacy, but Charlie panics when he thinks about kissing Alice. He has a flashback memory of his mother beating him brutally for having an erection. Alice kisses Charlie, but he seizes with terror and cries himself to sleep.

ANALYSIS: PROGRESS REPORTS 10–11

In this section we witness Charlie's intellectual growth continue unabated. He eventually surpasses everyone around him and starts to view and judge people with a more critical eye. Whereas on April 1 Charlie surprises his coworkers by demonstrating mere competence on the dough mixer, by April 21 he is redesigning the entire dough-mixing process. His intelligence is no longer merely mechanical. Charlie makes a tremendous psychological leap with his realization that he is capable of solving moral dilemmas, such as Gimpy's embezzlement, by himself. Now on a level intellectual playing field with those around him, Charlie perceives that they are not the titanic, impressive figures he once thought. Just as they are unimpressed with his new intellect, he is disappointed by their limitations, insecurities, and shortcomings.

Charlie comes to understand that the scientists, especially Professor Nemur, think of him as a laboratory specimen, not a real person or individual. Nemur's remark about Charlie being an "inanimate object" before the operation implies that Nemur thinks he alone has granted Charlie his humanity. Though Charlie deeply resents the assertion that he was not a real person before the surgery, even he does not feel entirely connected to his past. In fact, when he thinks back on his past—something he does constantly in these sections, deluged by a flood of memories—he sees himself from an external perspective, as "Charlie" rather than "I." Though Charlie's view of his former self could be compared to a doctor's view of a patient, Charlie nonetheless remains surprised by Nemur's clinical lack of compassion.

Earlier, Charlie had begun to understand how ostracized he was as a mentally retarded man, but he now sees that his superior intelligence brings him equal scorn. People who are accustomed to the old Charlie are unnerved by the change in him. Charlie recovers a memory of Gimpy being kind to him in the past, but now Gimpy joins the other workers to get Charlie fired. Gimpy regrets having been nice to Charlie, and even feels that he has wasted his compassion on someone who does not need or deserve it. Mr. Donner no longer feels the need to protect or shelter Charlie. Even Fanny, the only bakery worker who has consistently treated Charlie with kindness, now fears that his intellectual leap cannot be a pure blessing.

Charlie's intelligence also bothers people who never knew him before, such as the professors who shy away from intellectual discussions when they realize that Charlie has a greater depth of knowledge than they do. In his first progress reports, Charlie writes of a desire to "get smart" in order to make "frends," since he longs for normalcy. But now the experiment has taken Charlie's mental abilities too far. His genius is as much of a social curse as his mental retardation was earlier. Indeed, in this section Charlie seems torn between two unpleasant worlds, bothered by the dull college students he meets but still terribly saddened to lose his job at the bakery, a place that no longer has anything to offer him but familiarity.

As he grows closer to Alice, whom he no longer calls "Miss Kinnian"—another mark of his growing independence—Charlie recovers a number of memories that relate to sexuality and shame. He remembers intense trauma upon discovering Norma's bloody underpants in the laundry, and associates menstruation with violence and shame. Charlie remembers his mother beating him brutally upon finding him with an erection. Rose, tormented by Charlie's abnormality, sought to deny him his sexual desires, seemingly asserting that sexuality's inherent shamefulness could be eliminated only by a normal social existence. Since Rose assumed that Charlie could never have a fully normal social existence, she irrationally tried to beat his sexuality out of him. Charlie's struggle to break through the sexual panic Rose has instilled in him eventually becomes central to his struggle to overcome the difficulties of his past and live like a mature adult.

SUMMARY & ANALYSIS

PROGRESS REPORT 12

SUMMARY

I'll stop studying, and I'll be a dummy just like him.
I'll forget everything I learned and then I'll be just
like him. (See QUOTATIONS, p. 48)

Charlie writes that his relationship with Nemur is growing increasingly strained, as Nemur continues to treat him more as a laboratory specimen than a human being. Nemur is upset that Charlie has fallen behind on writing his progress reports. Charlie argues that the reports are too time-consuming and that he does not have enough time to learn about the outside world if he has to engage in constant self-analysis. Strauss suggests that Charlie learn to type, so he does.

Charlie has nightmares for three nights after his panic in Alice's apartment. He has a recurring image of a bakery window and of his former mentally retarded self on the other side of the pane, watching him. He remembers a childhood incident in which Norma, who had gotten an A on a test, asked their mother for a dog that she had promised if Norma did well in school. Charlie had offered to help take care of the dog if their parents bought one for Norma, but Norma had demanded that the dog be hers alone. Charlie and Norma's father had declared that if Norma was going to be so selfish about it, there would be no dog, despite Rose's promise. Norma resentfully threatened to "forget" everything she knew and be a "dummy" like Charlie if her good work would not be rewarded. Angrily, Charlie now wishes he could tell Norma that he never intended to hurt or annoy her, but that he only wanted her to like him and play with him.

Charlie goes to visit Alice in her classroom at the Center for Retarded Adults and sees many of the mentally disabled people with whom he had once attended the school. Alice is upset that Charlie has come into the classroom and tells him that he is no longer the warm, open person she once knew, that he has grown cold and aggressive. Charlie insists that he has merely learned to defend himself. Alice replies that she now feels insecure around Charlie because of his clear intellectual superiority. He drops Alice off at her apartment, feeling sad, angry, and very distant from her. His love, he thinks, has cooled into fondness. As his intelligence has skyrocketed, his affection for Alice has diminished.

Charlie picks up the habit of wandering through the streets of New York at night. One night, he meets a strange and sad woman in Central Park who tells him about her problems and then offers to have sex with him. Charlie almost goes home with the woman, until she reveals that she is pregnant. Charlie flashes back to an image of his mother pregnant with his sister, which he associates with his mother beginning to give up on him and placing her hopes in Norma instead. Cursing the woman in the park, Charlie grabs her shoulder. She screams, and a group of people runs toward them. Charlie runs away, and he hears the woman tell the group that he tried to attack her. Part of Charlie longs to be caught and beaten. He wants to be punished, though he cannot say why or for what.

Analysis

Charlie's intellectual journey continues in this section, but now Keyes only hints at the outward manifestations of Charlie's genius. Instead, Charlie's inward journey becomes his focus and, thus, the focus of the novel. Alice notes this trend, telling Charlie she does not understand his talk about "cultural variants, and neo-Boulean mathematics, and post-symbolic logic." She now associates him with these complex terms and ideas, reflecting her inability to relate to him now that he is off in his own world. Charlie now studies his own emotions much as he has studied grammar, Shakespeare, economics, and other academic pursuits. As he walks home from his upsetting encounter with Alice, he seems to analyze his emotions even as he is going through them.

Charlie's belief that his love for Alice is inversely related to his level of mental ability indicates a conflict between intellect and emotion. This conflict is also embodied in the opposing characters of Nemur and Alice. Professor Nemur, an obsessive, career-driven academic determined to make a name for himself as a great scientist, represents one extreme—the idea that intelligence is everything in human life. Nemur believes that nothing besides intellect matters and that mental disability makes an individual less than human. Alice, as a compassionate and generous teacher of disabled adults, represents the opposite perspective—the idea that kindness and feeling are more important than intelligence. Both Nemur and Alice frustrate Charlie, Nemur because of his arrogant dismissal of Charlie's former life, and Alice because of her disinterest in Charlie's new mental powers. Charlie struggles to find a balance between these two perspectives throughout the rest of the novel and searches for a way to combine his superhuman intelligence with human feeling without betraying either.

Charlie's childhood memory of Norma and the dog puts forth the idea that intelligence is not the most important human trait, but does so in a sarcastic fashion. When Norma is denied her dog because of her refusal to share it with Charlie, she concludes that Charlie is getting preferential treatment because of his disability. She threatens to "lose" all of her intelligence—a feat just as impossible as Charlie gaining intelligence—in order to receive treatment equal to Charlie's. This idea is a curious reversal of the pattern of condescension toward the mentally disabled, as in this moment, Norma does not feel superior to Charlie but envious of him. Keyes reinforces the notion that superior intelligence does not necessarily lead to a superior capacity for happiness.

Charlie's struggle is complicated by his burgeoning sexual desire, which comes into direct conflict with his ingrained sense of shame and self-loathing associated with sexuality. Though Charlie's newfound intelligence helps him gain understanding about why he feels so confused about sex, he still cannot control his turmoil. When the woman in the park offers to make love to Charlie, he is initially prepared to take her up on her offer. When he kisses her, he does not experience the extreme paralyzing hallucinations that he has had in similar situations with Alice. Keyes implies that in removing the emotional aspects of intimacy, Charlie may be approaching sex more clinically and learning more about the act and himself in the process. However, Charlie's hope of uncomplicated sex is shattered by the woman's revelation that she is pregnant, and his resultant flashback to his pregnant mother brings back all of the searing shame and panic he hopes to avoid. The suddenness of the shame Charlie feels makes it seem particularly acute, even stronger than the shame he feels earlier with Alice. In hoping to be caught and beaten by the crowd that thinks he has tried to rape the woman, Charlie links desire with punishment—exactly what his mother ingrained in him. Charlie's intellect has been catapulted to dizzying heights, but nothing can be done to make his emotional development keep pace.

PROGRESS REPORT 13

SUMMARY

Step right this way and see the side show! An act never before seen in the scientific world! A mouse and a moron turned into geniuses before your very eyes!
(See QUOTATIONS, p. 49)

Charlie begins dictating his progress reports to a tape recorder. The first part of this report is recorded on a flight to Chicago, where Nemur and Strauss are scheduled to reveal their preliminary findings at a scientific convention. Charlie and Algernon will be the star exhibits of the presentation. As the plane takes off, Charlie is uncomfortable putting his seat belt on because he dislikes the feeling of confinement. Trying to remember why, he flashes back to a time in childhood when his mother took him to a quack doctor named Guarino, who promised to increase Charlie's intelligence to a normal level. This visit took place before Norma was born, when Rose's energies were still primarily focused on making Charlie normal. Though Charlie's father was skeptical, Rose insisted that Charlie go through with Guarino's regimen, which included being strapped onto a table. This claustrophobic procedure instilled in Charlie a fear of confinement. Though Guarino was a crook and his process a sham, Charlie bears him no ill will—Guarino was always kind to him and never made him feel inferior for his disability. Charlie also remembers that his father harbored bitterness about the expensive therapy sessions, as they forced him to continue working as a barbershop-supply salesman, postponing his longtime dream of opening his own barbershop. By the time the plane lands, Charlie no longer feels uncomfortable in his seat belt.

At the hotel before the conference, Charlie meets many curious scientists and students who have heard about him. They engage him on a wide variety of topics, and his vast range of knowledge enables him to discuss with ease everything from contemporary economic theory to obscure linguistics and mathematics. When Charlie hears Nemur discussing the experiment with a student, the student asks Nemur about an article recently published in the *Hindu Journal of Psychopathology* on related scientific matters. Charlie is shocked to learn that Nemur did not read the article because he does not speak Hindi. Charlie is further stunned to learn that Strauss does not speak Hindi either. Strauss claims to speak six different languages, but that number is unimpressive to Charlie, who has learned more languages than that in just the past two months. Charlie realizes that he now understands more about the experiment than Nemur and Strauss, and he storms away, angrily declaring that they are frauds. Burt catches Charlie and urges him to be more tolerant of others' shortcomings, especially since Nemur and Strauss have never claimed to be all-knowing. Charlie understands that he has been impatient and realizes that his quest to take in all of the world's knowledge is an impossible one.

Charlie sits on the stage during Nemur and Strauss's presentation. Listening to Burt deliver his paper about Algernon, Charlie learns that Algernon's behavior grew erratic and self-destructive at the height of his intelligence. Charlie is annoyed that this information has been withheld from him. He also grows increasingly frustrated at hearing the scientists suggest that he was subhuman prior to their operation and feels like a debased carnival sideshow act. Charlie privately toys with the idea of creating havoc in the convention by letting Algernon out of his cage.

During Nemur's remarks, Charlie suddenly realizes that there is a scientific flaw in the experiment: Nemur and Strauss have miscalculated the amount of observation time necessary to determine whether or not Algernon's increased intelligence will be permanent. Charlie realizes that he may yet lose his intelligence. Angry with Nemur now both for his patronizing attitude and for his lack of scientific thoroughness, Charlie succumbs to his urge to free Algernon from his cage. As the mouse scampers away, the auditorium descends into chaos. Charlie is able to catch Algernon, and he runs away from the conference with the mouse in his pocket. He catches a flight back to New York, where he plans to find an apartment and hide from Strauss and Nemur for a while. A new sense of urgency falls upon Charlie with the knowledge that his intelligence may desert him.

ANALYSIS

Charlie's sudden realization that his intelligence may soon falter and his subsequent flight from the convention form the climax of the novel's first half. Up to this point, Charlie's struggle has been to establish and trust his own independence after having been conditioned his entire life to believe that he is inferior. Charlie is not immediately able to accept that his intelligence qualifies him to make his own decisions. Even when angered by the shortcomings of those around him, he has been reluctant to break from the structured environment of the lab. Some part of Charlie has continued to believe that he needs to be directed and controlled, just as his mother sought to control him. However, Charlie's attitude changes when he abandons the scientists at the convention, finally cutting his ties to any outside authority.

Charlie's willingness to trust himself results, in part, from his discovery that his mental abilities have come further than imagined. In the beginning of the novel, the retarded Charlie associates becoming smart with becoming normal. But Charlie's development has been so rapid that he has not had the time or perspective to gauge what normalcy really is. Though there have been indications that Charlie's intelligence has leapfrogged well above average—for example, his growing impatience with the Beekman professors he meets, and Alice's remark that she cannot keep up with his academic interests—his realization that he is now smarter than Nemur and Strauss nonetheless comes as a nerve-wracking revelation. When Charlie discovers that Nemur cannot speak Hindi, his first reaction is to label Nemur a fraud, even though Nemur has certainly never claimed to speak Hindi. In actuality, what Charlie perceives as fraudulent is the notion that Nemur is superior to him, a notion that Charlie can now trust himself to deny.

As Charlie comes to grips with the fact that his intellect and knowledge are greater than that of the people who are studying him, he readjusts his criteria for judging them personally. Since Charlie is now the intellectual equal of the scientists he meets, they no longer seem godlike or impressive, and he now judges them by their capacity for compassion. Charlie's flashbacks to the treatments by the quack Dr. Guarino illustrate his new value system. Charlie thinks well of Guarino because, though he was a crook and an impostor, he was always kind. Guarino stands in stark contrast to Nemur, who is accomplished and perhaps brilliant in his field, but also arrogant and dismissive of Charlie.

Charlie's feeling of identification with Algernon becomes more acute in this section. Charlie initially feels like Algernon's competitor, but ever since surpassing Algernon's maze-solving ability, he feels that he is, in a sense, Algernon's protector. Feeling like a sideshow on the convention stage, Charlie develops a strong sympathy for Algernon, locked in his cage. Charlie resents that the mouse has to solve puzzles for his food, just as he resents the way that he himself is trotted out for the entertainment of the callous scientists. Charlie's letting Algernon out of his cage symbolically frees Charlie from Nemur and Strauss's observation.

Keyes uses the end of this section to set up great suspense for the rest of the novel. Charlie's realization that Nemur's hypothesis is flawed and that he and Algernon may both lose their intelligence thrusts us again into the position of doctors reading Charlie's progress reports. However, unlike the beginning of the novel, when we are cued to look for signs of increased intelligence, Keyes now puts us on alert for signs of decreased mental ability. We—and Charlie—sense the need to watch Algernon carefully, because of the ominous suggestion that whatever happens to Algernon will happen to Charlie in turn.

PROGRESS REPORTS 14–15

SUMMARY: PROGRESS REPORT 14

> *I wasn't his son. That was another Charlie.*
> *Intelligence and knowledge had changed me, and he*
> *would resent me. . . .*   (See QUOTATIONS, p. 50)

Charlie sees a newspaper article that contains an interview with Norma, in which Norma insists she does not know Charlie's whereabouts. Charlie learns that his mother told Norma that he had been sent off to the Warren State Home, an institution for the mentally disabled, and had died there years ago. Charlie also reads that his father now owns his own barbershop and no longer lives with his mother. Charlie recalls that after Norma's birth, Rose had stopped longing for him to become normal and had started wanting him to disappear.

Charlie moves into an apartment in the city. He builds Algernon an elaborate maze to solve and meets his neighbor Fay Lillman, a free-spirited and flirtatious artist. Fay is appalled by the neatness of Charlie's apartment, saying she cannot stand straight lines and that she drinks to make the lines go blurry. Charlie finds Fay strange but undeniably attractive.

Charlie visits his father at his barbershop. Matt does not recognize his son, and treats him as a customer. Too nervous to say anything, Charlie gets a haircut. He remembers the night that his father took him to live with his Uncle Herman after Rose had become hysterical, threatening that she would kill Charlie with a carving knife if he were not shipped out to the Warren State Home immediately. Charlie attempts to reveal his identity to Matt, but after an awkward and inconclusive exchange, he gives up and leaves the shop.

Algernon performs well in Charlie's new mazes but sometimes appears to be angry or depressed, frenetically throwing himself against the walls. Fay buys Algernon a female companion mouse named Minnie. Fay stays in Charlie's apartment one night. They have drinks together and Charlie passes out. The next morning, naked in bed together, Fay says that they have not made love and wonders whether Charlie is gay. She tells him that he acted like a little kid while he was drunk. Charlie realizes that the old, mentally retarded Charlie has not left him and that his former self still exists within his mind.

Charlie spends a day in movie theaters and wandering the streets, just to be among other people. He eats at the diner where he took Alice after their movie date. A mentally disabled busboy accidentally breaks some dishes, and as he sweeps up the mess, the customers taunt him cruelly. Not comprehending that he is the target of the customers' mockery, the busboy smiles along with their insults. Charlie is infuriated and screams to the crowd that the busboy is human and deserves respect.

Charlie visits Alice and talks over his feelings with her. He worries that he has become emotionally detached from everyone around him, and he yearns to reconnect with humanity. Charlie wonders if the inner, mentally retarded Charlie would allow him to make love to Alice if he pretended that she were Fay. He hypothesizes that since he cares for Fay less deeply than he does for Alice, his inner self might not panic at the notion of sex with Fay. Charlie turns out the lights and begins kissing Alice but is unable to trick himself into believing that she is Fay, and he feels guilty for trying to use her in an emotional experiment.

Charlie goes home and waits for Fay to return from dancing. When she arrives, he is sexually aggressive. They make love, and he senses the "other" Charlie watching them but not panicking. Charlie and Fay begin an affair, and he soon loses the sense of the other Charlie's surveillance. Charlie decides to go back to the lab and take over research on the experiment. One day Algernon attacks Minnie and bites Fay. Charlie is concerned by Algernon's hostility.

SUMMARY: PROGRESS REPORT 15

The Welberg Foundation, which is paying for the experiment, agrees to allow Charlie to work at Beekman without having to report to Nemur. Charlie returns to the lab, and Burt begins working with Algernon again. He is disturbed to discover that Algernon's problem-solving abilities seem to have regressed. Charlie asks Nemur what contingency plans have been made for him if his own intelligence should not hold. Nemur tells him that should he become retarded again, he will be sent to the Warren State Home. Charlie decides that he needs to visit Warren to see what may await him.

ANALYSIS: PROGRESS REPORTS 14–15

Charlie's anticlimactic visit with his father brings into focus his notion that there are two Charlie Gordons, the former mentally disabled simpleton and the current genius. This idea has been implicit in Charlie's dreams and hallucinations but only now becomes apparent and real to him. Though Matt has never been strong enough to fully defend Charlie against Rose's tyranny, he has always supported his son, and for that reason Charlie feels warmly toward his father. Charlie is unable to bring himself to reveal his identity to Matt because he knows that he is no longer the Charlie Matt once knew. Just as the bakery workers are not proud of Charlie's new intellect, Charlie fears that Matt will have no reason to feel anything but threatened by his genius son.

Charlie's relationship with Fay represents a step forward in his personal and emotional development. Fay is the first significant character in the novel who does not know that Charlie used to be mentally disabled. Though Charlie has mentioned brief interactions with professors at Beekman who do not know about his past, Fay is the first new acquaintance with whom he allows himself to have a personal relationship. Fay is unlike anyone else in his world: when she talks about her loathing of straight lines, it implies that she is entirely uninterested in the world of science and intellectual pursuits. Fay's odd way of being is purely emotional, and she is thus an appropriate teacher for the emotionally crippled Charlie.

Though Charlie realizes in this section that emotional troubles cannot be solved in the same manner as intellectual puzzles, he nonetheless maintains a scientific approach to his emotional development. He observes his own behavior in a number of sexually tense situations in an attempt to determine what is causing his confusion. Much as Burt might conduct an experiment by building different mazes for Algernon, Charlie constructs different sexually charged situations to see how the *other* Charlie will react. While the other Charlie objects violently to the prospect of intimacy with Alice, he is merely curious about intimacy with Fay. This difference may arise from the fact that the old Charlie does not know Fay and does not have the residual feelings of overwhelming love for her that he has for Alice. Charlie's attempt to make love to Alice while pretending she is Fay is, in effect, an experiment to see if the other Charlie can be tricked into calmness. However, Charlie is unable to go through with his experiment because he realizes that doing so would be tantamount to treating Alice as an inhuman, scientific factor, just as Nemur had callously treated him.

Keyes strengthens the parallel between Charlie and Algernon by introducing Minnie, a female companion for Algernon, around the same time that Charlie begins his affair with Fay. However, Algernon's increasingly erratic behavior is a frightening omen of what lies ahead for Charlie. Algernon's attack on Minnie creates suspense by leading us to wonder if Charlie will soon lash out at Fay, or even at Alice. When we learn that Algernon's intelligence has already begun to desert him, we know that Charlie's decline cannot be far off. The other Charlie, the Charlie from the beginning of the novel, is waiting in the wings to reassert himself.

PROGRESS REPORT 16

SUMMARY

Charlie visits the Warren Home. The staff makes a good impression on him, but the residents' poor conditions and dim faces upset him, as he imagines that he will soon be among them. Charlie is particularly distressed by an encounter with a friendly deaf-mute boy. Charlie has difficulty mustering kindness in a moment when the boy seems to seek his approval.

Alice visits Charlie's apartment one night, and Fay unexpectedly shows up. To Charlie's surprise, the two women get along favorably, and they all stay up late talking and drinking. Alice tells Charlie that she understands why he is enamored with Fay's lightheartedness and spontaneity but worries that Fay and her drinking habits are detrimental to Charlie's important work. Charlie makes love to Fay, thinking all along about Alice. He immerses himself increasingly in his work, often sleeping at the lab. Fay moves on to another boyfriend, but Charlie cannot be distracted, and he is exhilarated by the intensity of his own concentration. Algernon's condition continues to deteriorate, and Charlie knows that if he can figure out the cause, he will give the world knowledge that could be invaluable to future research.

Charlie attends a party in honor of the Welberg Foundation. He overhears Strauss explaining to a foundation board member that even failed experiments are scientifically valuable, for they are often as educational as successes. Somewhat drunk, Charlie starts to interject a rude comment, but Strauss cuts him off. Charlie continues to alienate the guests, and when the party is over, Nemur accuses Charlie of being ungrateful for all that the operation has given him. Charlie argues that he has little for which to be grateful, since he feels that the greatest lesson he has learned with his intelligence is that people scorn him whether he is a moron or a genius.

Nemur accuses Charlie of becoming cynical and self-centered. In his drunken and emotional state, Charlie senses himself starting to act like the mentally retarded Charlie. He hurries to the bathroom and looks in the mirror, and he feels that he is looking directly at the other Charlie. He tells the other Charlie that they are enemies and that he will fight to keep the retarded Charlie from regaining control of his body. He goes home miserable, deciding that Nemur's accusations have been correct.

Charlie soon has a massive intellectual breakthrough and writes a paper on his findings. In a letter to Nemur, he explains that he has uncovered a phenomenon he deems the "Algernon-Gordon Effect," which argues that the more artificially induced intelligence one gains, the quicker it will deteriorate. Charlie tries to reassure Nemur and Strauss, as well as a distraught Alice, that they could not have foreseen this effect and should not feel guilty. Charlie senses that he is becoming absentminded, the first hint of the onset of his decline. Algernon soon dies, and Charlie buries him in the backyard, putting flowers on the grave.

Charlie goes to see his mother. Rose panics, and Charlie tries to win her trust, frantically telling her as much as he can about what has happened to him. He quickly realizes that his mother is delusional: though at one moment she seems to understand that he is her son, the next she asks him if he is a bill collector. Charlie patiently tries to explain his recent progress, telling Rose that he has fulfilled her dreams and become a success. He gives her the paper he has written in an attempt to make her happy. Rose is proud and feels vindicated. Norma, now an adult caring for Rose, arrives home. To Charlie's surprise, she is delighted to see him. They have a long talk, and Norma apologizes for having been cruel to Charlie when they were children. The peace is suddenly broken when Rose comes at Charlie with a knife, telling him to keep away from Norma with his sexual thoughts. Charlie leaves in tears. As he walks away, he looks back at the house and sees the face of his boyhood self peering through the window.

ANALYSIS

As Charlie feels increased pressure to make the most of his intellect before it deserts him, he focuses on two goals intensely. First, he wishes to untangle the scientific mystery of why his intellect will regress. Second, he longs to attain some degree of emotional maturity, especially in terms of his relationships with Alice and Fay. Though intellect and emotion have often seemed to be in conflict throughout the novel, these two quests are intertwined in this section. Charlie's immersion in Fay's lifestyle of dance, drink, and sex has been significant to his development, but he immediately forsakes Fay for the laboratory when Alice suggests that his work is too important to be compromised by distractions. Despite Charlie's assertion in Progress Report 12 that his love for Alice has dissipated, she remains the person with whom he has the strongest emotional bond. It is Alice's encouragement alone that allows Charlie to recognize that his relationship with Fay is not the whole of his emotional being, and that he can focus on his work without giving up his emotional quest. Intellectual work *becomes* emotional for Charlie; his scientific breakthroughs fill him with joy in a way they previously could not.

Charlie has felt bitterness toward Nemur for most of the novel, but Nemur is never able to rebut Charlie's accusations until their argument after the cocktail party. The points Nemur makes are strong enough to alter Charlie's perception completely. Nemur reminds Charlie that he was an entirely different person before the operation—not merely mentally retarded, but also kindhearted and warm. Though Nemur may take credit for making Charlie intelligent, he takes no credit at all for creating the new cold and unpleasant Charlie. This new, cold personality, Nemur suggests, is Charlie's own creation. Charlie's complaint that Nemur is appallingly arrogant and inconsiderate remains essentially valid. However, Charlie realizes that he has come to embody these qualities himself and that, despite his extraordinary circumstances, he has no better excuse for these traits than Nemur does. This realization marks Charlie's greatest leap toward emotional maturity. Though he still carries a frightened boy within, after the argument with Nemur he comes to take full responsibility for his own life.

It is this new sense of responsibility and independence that gives Charlie the strength to see his mother and sister, an experience that completes his struggle to come to terms with his past. Whereas Charlie is earlier unable to reveal his true identity to his father, here he insists on doing so to his mother. Charlie persists in trying to make his mother understand who he is and what has happened to him, despite the difficulty of reaching her through her dementia. Charlie patiently retells the story until his mother understands, as it is crucial for him to know that he has done his best to reconnect with her on some level. Given Rose's delusional state, all Charlie can do is try to make her happy. He does so by acting out the irrational fantasy Rose has harbored since Charlie's youth: the idea of his development into normalcy and success.

Charlie's reunion with Norma is more satisfying emotionally for him. In their conversation, Charlie grasps some of Norma's perspective on their shared youth, and he is able to empathize with her. Though the wounds of Charlie's childhood can never be fully healed, his new understanding of his mother and sister enables him to forgive them. With time running out before his intelligence recedes, Charlie unshackles himself from the emotional burden of his past.

PROGRESS REPORT 17

SUMMARY

> *Its easy to have frends if you let pepul laff at you. Im going to have lots of frends where I go.*
>
> (See QUOTATIONS, p. 51)

Charlie contemplates suicide but decides he must keep writing his reports for the sake of science. At a therapy session with Strauss, Charlie has a hallucination in which he seems to fly into the center of his own unconscious, represented by a red, pulsing flower, and then imagines himself being battered against the walls of a cave.

When Burt tests Charlie on his ability to solve mazes in the lab, Charlie has difficulty and gets frustrated. Charlie then finds himself perplexed by the Rorschach test. He tells Burt that he will no longer come to the lab.

Strauss tries to visit Charlie at his apartment, but Charlie refuses to let him in. Charlie picks up his copy of *Paradise Lost,* and though he knows he loved the book only a few months before, he is now unable to understand it. He flashes back to a time when his mother, frustratedly trying to teach him to read, had insisted to his father that Charlie was not retarded but merely lazy. Charlie tears the copy of *Paradise Lost* apart.

Alice comes to stay with Charlie. She says she wants to spend as much time as possible with him before the effects of the operation recede completely. She holds him, and for once he does not feel the old inner panic. They make love for the first time, and it is a transcendent, spiritual experience, unlike the purely physical sex Charlie has had with Fay. Despite their happiness, Charlie cannot bear the thought of Alice witnessing his descent. He tells Alice that he will probably ask her to leave soon, and he makes her promise that when she does leave, she will never come back.

Charlie picks up his paper on the Algernon-Gordon Effect and is unable to understand it. He can no longer remember the languages he taught himself. His motor control begins to deteriorate, and he finds himself watching television all day. Alice tries to help by tidying up Charlie's apartment, but her actions anger him because he wants everything left as it is, "to remind me of what I'm leaving behind." Charlie also gets upset at Alice for trying to encourage him to pursue intellectual activities in which he is no longer interested. Alice's denial of Charlie's condition reminds him of his mother. He asks Alice to leave and, devastated, she does.

Charlie wonders if he can stall his deterioration. He knows that he cannot keep himself from forgetting things, but wonders if he can still learn and retain new things, thus maintaining a steady level of intelligence. However, in his entry of November 1, Charlie's punctuation is flawed, and soon he loses accuracy in grammar and spelling as well. He describes voyeuristically watching a woman bathing in the apartment across the courtyard. Alice comes to see Charlie but he refuses to let her in.

Having regressed almost completely to his original state, Charlie returns to the Donner's Bakery and gets his old job back. He refuses to accept money from Alice and Strauss. When a new employee named Meyer Klaus picks on Charlie and threatens to break his arm, Joe, Frank, and Gimpy come to Charlie's rescue. They tell him that he should come to them for help if anyone ever gives him trouble. Charlie is grateful for his friends.

Charlie forgets that he is no longer enrolled in Alice's class at the Center for Retarded Adults and shows up for one of the meetings. When Alice sees Charlie has reverted entirely to his original state, she runs from the room weeping. Charlie senses that people feel sorry for him, and he decides to go live at the Warren Home. In his final note, he says that he is glad he got to be smart for a short time and that he got to learn about his family. He has a vague memory of himself as a genius: "he looks different and he walks different but I dont think its me because its like I see him from the window." He writes goodbye to Alice and Dr. Strauss, and advises Professor Nemur that he will have more friends if he does not get so upset when people laugh at him. Finally, Charlie leaves a postscript requesting "please if you get a chanse put some flowrs on Algernons grave in the bak yard."

ANALYSIS

Just as Keyes creates suspense as we wait for Charlie's intellectual ability to increase, here we anxiously watch for signs of Charlie's regression. Charlie's fight to maintain his intelligence increases this suspense, as we wonder whether he can forestall his descent by attempting to learn and replace the knowledge he is losing. We retain hope that Charlie might be able to maintain average intelligence. Keyes dashes this hope almost immediately as the poor punctuation of the next entry demonstrates Charlie's worst mental slippage yet. We are soon reading the prose of the reports' original narrator, the mentally disabled Charlie. The jarring dissimilarity of the two writing styles reinforces the notion that there are two Charlies, and that the original has returned to stay. This old, slower Charlie retains a piece of the genius Charlie in his memory. The image of Charlie seeing his old self through the metaphorical window is reversed: the old Charlie now views the genius Charlie, just as the genius Charlie earlier views the old Charlie peering in at him.

The genius Charlie exits the novel on a bittersweet note. His affair with Alice, in his last days of heightened intellect, is the peak of his emotional development. Having overcome his association of sex with shame, Charlie is finally able to see Alice as an emotional equal. No longer afraid of Alice's womanhood or her sexual impulses, and no longer feeling the gaze of the other Charlie, he is able to consummate the romance that he feels has always existed. When Charlie says that the love he and Alice experience is "more than most people find in a lifetime," we know that he has accomplished his loftiest goal—emotional fulfillment.

The completeness of Charlie's intellectual regression implies that nothing has been gained. However, Charlie has grown emotionally in the novel, and this growth will stay with him forever. He has Nemur and Strauss to thank for his brief term as a genius, but his emotional fulfillment has been his own achievement. At the end, Charlie writes that he is glad to have learned about his family and that he feels he is "a person just like evryone." We see that, though his detailed memories of childhood may leave him, his sense of understanding and forgiveness toward his family have remained.

Though Charlie is warmhearted at the beginning of the novel, his return to this state is not mere regression. He has traveled through bitterness and isolation, and his warmth now resonates not from emotional simplicity but from meaningful experience. Charlie will not be the same: like Adam and Eve—the subjects of John Milton's poem *Paradise Lost,* a work the genius Charlie loved—Charlie has seen and learned too much to return to his original state unchanged. Though he has feared and hated the Warren Home throughout the novel, he believes that he will be content there at the end.

Charlie has always approached his reports as purposeful for educational or research reasons, so he uses a postscript to Nemur to teach a lesson. In the previous report, Nemur accuses Charlie of becoming cold as he has become brilliant, and Charlie realizes that Nemur is right. Now, Charlie attempts to return the favor by teaching Nemur the same lesson that Nemur has taught him: that if he opens his heart he will "have more frends." Keyes leaves a glimmer of hope that not only will Charlie's reports be valuable for science's sake, but perhaps Nemur and others will be able to glean emotional wisdom from them.

Charlie's final postscript is also telling. Algernon, like any laboratory animal, was chosen for the experiment not for personal qualities but as a representative of the behavior of all mice. By asking the researchers to put fresh flowers on Algernon's grave, Charlie frames Algernon as an individual, not a scientific subject. By asking the scientists to respect the mouse's memory as he respects it, Charlie demonstrates that he has retained his own sense of self-worth.

IMPORTANT QUOTATIONS EXPLAINED

1. And he said that meens Im doing something grate for
    sience and Ill be famus and my name will go down in
    the books. I dont care so much about beeing famus. I
    just want to be smart like other pepul so I can have
    lots of frends who like me.

Here, in his "progris riport 6th," Charlie recounts a conversation he has with Nemur shortly before his operation. Nemur cannot guarantee that Charlie's procedure will be successful, but he is trying to make Charlie feel good about his participation in the experiment nonetheless. Nemur's attempts to impress Charlie with promises of fame and great contributions to science reveal his true motivations. It is Nemur who wants his name to "go down in the books," not Charlie. On the contrary, Charlie's reason for wanting to be intelligent is purely social: he wants people to like him. Charlie knows that his retardation has cut him off from most of society, but his powerlessness does not upset him. Charlie does not long to join society to increase his social standing; rather, he longs to join primarily because he is lonely. In Charlie's mind, intelligence is the quality that will gain him entry into a world of friends. The resulting irony is that when Charlie does become incredibly intelligent, he finds himself even lonelier than before.

2. "And I hate school! I hate it! I'll stop studying, and I'll be a dummy like him. I'll forget everything I learned and then I'll be just like him." She runs out of the room, shrieking: "It's happening to me already. I'm forgetting everything . . . I'm forgetting . . . I don't remember anything I learned any more!"

This passage, from Progress Report 12, is part of one of Charlie's flashbacks to his childhood, in this case the incident when Norma demands her parents give her a dog because she has received an A on her history exam. After her father denies Norma the dog because she refuses to allow Charlie to help care for it, Norma angrily threatens her parents. She feels that Charlie is getting preferential treatment because he is retarded, and she suggests that perhaps she should become a "dummy" like him to receive the same treatment. Though Norma is clearly being absurd and sarcastic, for a moment it seems that she genuinely envies Charlie's retardation—the only time in the novel when anyone perceives Charlie's disability as an advantage. Listening to Norma rant, however, Charlie can hardly feel that he is in an enviable position. His disability, which he cannot help, makes his sister miserable.

Norma's threat to lose her intelligence is meant to be just as ludi-crous as the notion that Charlie could gain intelligence by his own will. Of course, many years later, Charlie does in fact gain intelli-gence. Norma's remark—"I don't remember anything I learned any more!"—is a cruel joke meant to upset her parents, but it also fore-shadows exactly what happens to Charlie at the end of the novel.

3. We were the main attraction of the evening, and when
    we settled, the chairman began his introduction. I half
    expected to hear him boom out: *Laideezzz and
    gentulmennnnnn. Step right this way and see the side
    show! An act never before seen in the scientific world!
    A mouse and a moron turned into geniuses before
    your very eyes!*

This passage appears in Progress Report 13, when Charlie and
Algernon accompany Nemur and Strauss to the scientific convention in Chicago where they are presenting their findings. The
researchers treat Charlie and Algernon as exhibits, and Charlie
grows increasingly upset that he is being treated as more of a laboratory animal than a human being. At the convention, Charlie's
feeling of victimization reaches a new level of intensity. He is sur-
rounded by an entire auditorium of scientists who are curious to
see him not as an individual but merely as the result of Nemur and
Strauss's experiment. Charlie feels as though there are hundreds of
Nemurs all eyeing him clinically, and that he is there not so much
to enlighten the scientists as to entertain them. He imagines the
chairman of the conference as a carnival barker, touting Charlie
and Algernon as a "side show," the portion of the circus where so-
called freaks are put on display. Charlie imagines the chairman callously referring to him as a "moron," grotesquely proving that he
is not the least bit concerned with Charlie's feelings. This paranoid
fantasy is the height of Charlie's sense of being objectified; it leads
him to assert his independence by running away from the conference with Algernon.

QUOTATIONS

4.   I wasn't his son. That was another Charlie.
      Intelligence and knowledge had changed me, and he
      would resent me—as the others from the bakery
      resented me—because my growth diminished him. I
      didn't want that.

This passage comes from Progress Report 14, when Charlie goes to visit his father, Matt, hoping to talk with him and learn more about his own childhood. However, Matt does not recognize Charlie, and Charlie cannot bring himself to tell Matt who he really is. This reluctance emphasizes the feeling of split identity Charlie experiences as he grows smarter. When Charlie notes his intelligence increasing, he starts to have a sense that the "other" Charlie—his former mentally disabled self—watches over him, remaining present in the back of his mind. In this quotation, Charlie realizes why he feels he cannot and should not reveal his identity to Matt: Charlie is no longer that "other" self that he imagines, and therefore is no longer the same Charlie who was Matt's son.

Though Charlie longs to connect to and understand his past, he realizes that he has traveled too far to be able to present himself as the same person he used to be. He believes that rather than being happy for his son's massive gains in intelligence, Matt would feel betrayed if he were to discover that the articulate and bright man before him is Charlie. Charlie thinks that Matt would feel "diminished" by Charlie's intelligence, not just because Charlie is now far smarter than Matt is, but also because Matt invested so much energy into relating to his son as a mentally retarded boy. For years, Matt dealt with the difficulty of having a retarded son, and he also faced the greater difficulty of trying to persuade his irrational wife to accept Charlie's disability. Charlie fears that if a new, brilliant Charlie were to come along all these years later, Matt would feel that he had wasted all of his emotional energy and might even feel cheated. Charlie is effectively two people now, but neither person can have a whole life or a whole history.

5.   P.S. please tel prof Nemur not to be such a grouch
      when pepul laff at him and he would have more
      frends. Its easy to have frends if you let pepul laff at
      you. Im going to have lots of frends where I go.

These words constitute Charlie's second-to-last postscript in his
final progress report. Having decided to go live at the Warren State
Home and cut himself off from all the people he has known, Charlie
writes farewells to Alice and Dr. Strauss, but he saves a special word
of advice for Nemur. Throughout the novel, Nemur is portrayed as
a humorless and intensely career-focused man lacking in human
compassion. For a time, at the height of his genius, Charlie's own
intellectual self-absorption threatens to turn him into a similarly
cold individual. Upon discovering that his bakery coworkers used
to tease him for sport when he was mentally retarded, Charlie
becomes understandably angry and embittered, hating the idea that
he was the subject of such mockery.

Unlike Charlie, Nemur has not been the target of cruel jokes,
but he is nonetheless insecure and fears any challenge to his
authority. Near the end of the novel, Charlie comes to learn that
intellectual superiority is not the most important goal of a human
life. He is able to steer himself away from becoming like Nemur,
learning to love and forgive other people. Now, in this report, written after he has fully reverted to his original state, Charlie tries to
pass on some of what he has learned to Nemur. Although Charlie
is no longer capable of articulately expressing his emotional dis-
coveries to Nemur, his words nonetheless ring with the truth of
experience. Nemur would indeed have "more frends" if he were
not so focused on maintaining a pointless sense of superiority.
Charlie finds that, despite the vast intellectual gulf that separates
him from Nemur, the lessons he has learned apply just as much to
an esteemed scientific researcher as they do to a simpleminded man
confined by mental disability.

QUOTATIONS

KEY FACTS

FULL TITLE
Flowers for Algernon

AUTHOR
Daniel Keyes

TYPE OF WORK
Novel

GENRE
Science fiction

LANGUAGE
English

TIME AND PLACE WRITTEN
Original short story written in 1959, in New York City; expanded novel version written from 1962 to 1965 in New York and Ohio.

DATE OF FIRST PUBLICATION
Short story published in 1959; expanded novel form first published in 1966

PUBLISHER
Harcourt Brace Jovanovich

NARRATOR
Charlie Gordon, a mentally disabled man who undergoes experimental surgery to increase his intelligence

POINT OF VIEW
The novel is told in the form of first-person "progress reports" Charlie keeps throughout the course of the experiment. Everything is filtered through Charlie's mind, the capacities of which change drastically over the course of the novel, as Charlie's IQ triples and then plummets back to its original level.

TONE

The tone of the novel varies with Charlie's mental acuity. Sometimes, however—particularly when Charlie is writing as a retarded man at the beginning and end of the novel—Keyes allows him to provide hints in his narration that allow us to grasp the significance of events that Charlie cannot himself understand.

TENSE

Past; Charlie is always writing about the days he has just lived through. Charlie experiences numerous flashbacks to his childhood, which are usually narrated in the present tense.

SETTING (TIME)

There are no direct references to time period in the novel, but we can assume the events take place around the time the novel was written, the mid-1960s.

SETTING (PLACE)

New York City; one chapter takes place in Chicago

PROTAGONIST

Charlie Gordon

MAJOR CONFLICT

Charlie struggles to reach emotional maturity and feel like a whole person before his skyrocketing intelligence reverses course and returns him to his initial mentally disabled state.

RISING ACTION

Dr. Strauss performs an experimental surgery on Charlie that catapults his intelligence to genius levels; Charlie falls in love with Alice but finds he is unable to consummate their relationship because he feels unresolved childhood shame about his sexuality.

CLIMAX

Charlie asserts his independence by running away from the scientists who are observing him; Alice tells Charlie that his work at the laboratory is more important than his relationship with Fay; Charlie realizes in this moment that he can no longer run from his fate or the seriousness of his emotional journey.

KEY FACTS

FALLING ACTION

Charlie discovers the flaw in Nemur's hypothesis that proves that he will soon lose his intelligence; Charlie locates his mother and sister and is able to find forgive them for how they treated him as a child; Charlie has a brief, fulfilling romantic affair with Alice; Charlie returns to his original mentally retarded state and checks himself into the Warren State Home.

THEMES

Mistreatment of the mentally disabled; the tension between intellect and emotion; the persistence of the past in the present

MOTIFS

Changes in grammar, spelling, and punctuation; flashbacks; the scientific method

SYMBOLS

Algernon; Adam and Eve and the tree of knowledge; the window

FORESHADOWING

Professor Nemur tells Charlie at the outset of the experiment that his gains in intelligence may not be permanent, which turns out to be the case. Later, Charlie has a memory of his young sister, Norma, obnoxiously threatening to lose her own intelligence, another reference to Charlie's eventual downfall. Finally, Algernon's decline, beginning in Progress Report 13, is a reliable predictor of Charlie's impending deterioration.

STUDY QUESTIONS & ESSAY TOPICS

STUDY QUESTIONS

1. *What is the significance of Charlie's relationship to Fay? How does he feel about her? What role does their relationship play in his development?*

Though Charlie's romantic entanglement with Fay is short-lived, the lessons she teaches him about pure emotion and pure sex are a crucial stepping-stone in his development. Charlie struggles to reconcile his intellect and his emotions and longs to consummate his true love for Alice. Among the characters who are unaware of Charlie's history as a mentally retarded man, Fay is the only one with whom Charlie has a meaningful relationship. As such, she is the only person who is free to relate to Charlie without interference or influence from the "other" Charlie. After failing to consummate a burgeoning yet confusing romance with Alice, Charlie meets Fay and is amazed to discover how uncomplicated a sexual relationship can be. Charlie is not in love with Fay, but he is fond of and attracted to her, and since there is no history between them, he is able to put aside his impulsive feelings of shame and learn about very straightforward physical pleasures, such as drinking, dancing, and, most important, sex. Fay is smart but utterly nonintellectual—she does not care about the life of the mind and therefore is a perfect teacher for Charlie in his quest to learn about the emotional spectrum beyond his intellectual pursuits.

2. *Do you think that Charlie's writings as a mentally disabled man at the beginning and end of the novel accurately represent the way a disabled person genuinely might write? Defend your answer, and explain why you think these passages are written as they are.*

Keyes attempts to create a believably disabled character in the Charlie of the early progress reports. Charlie's grammatical errors are internally consistent and logically suggest the way a mentally retarded man might misconstrue the complex rules of the English language. Yet Keyes clearly takes artistic liberty with the tight structure of these reports—almost all of the information conveyed in these early segments is important to the plot that later develops. Charlie's ideas never seem scattered, and his thought process is never obscured by poor writing ability. What Keyes presents is thus not a strictly realistic portrayal of a retarded man's composition but makes for economical and exciting storytelling. Keyes often employs devices, such as Charlie's tendency early on to write down words he does not understand (like "PSYCHOLOGY LABORATORY"), that enable us to understand elements of Charlie's world that he himself does not. In these segments, Keyes strikes a delicate balance between making Charlie believable and keeping the narrative moving forward at a compelling pace.

3. *What is the role of memory in the novel? How do Charlie's flashbacks further the general themes of the novel?*

Throughout the novel, Charlie's gradually recovered memories of childhood tell a story that parallels the story that unfolds over the course of the experiment. As Charlie struggles to become emotionally independent and tries to form a deep bond with Alice, his memories shed light—for him and for us—on why this development is so difficult for him. Memories of his mother, Rose, instilling sexual shame in him arise when Charlie experiences this shame in the present. Likewise, Charlie's memories of being mistreated for his disability arise concurrently with his attempts to determine his new status in society. Charlie's increased intelligence enables him not only to recall things he has forgotten but also to understand the context of thoughts that earlier confused him. Charlie can see his past more clearly than he saw it while he was living it; in effect, he is learning about his past life as vividly and quickly as he is learning about his new life. The information Charlie garners from one life is always relevant to his grappling with the dilemmas of the other.

QUESTIONS & ESSAYS

SUGGESTED ESSAY TOPICS

1. How does the diary or journal-entry form of the novel affect the emphasis of the narrative? Is Charlie dependable as a narrator as he progresses through his various stages? Is Charlie capable of providing insight into the other characters, or is he too preoccupied with himself?

2. How has Charlie changed at the end of the novel? Is he different from the person he is at the beginning of the novel, and if so, how? Do you consider the novel's ending to be tragic or inspiring?

3. Does the novel make a definitive statement about the role of intelligence in human life, or does it simply explore this idea as an open-ended question?

4. Compare and contrast the characters of Professor Nemur and Dr. Strauss. How do their reactions to Charlie's intelligence differ? How do their approaches to science differ?

5. How does Algernon function as an alter ego for Charlie? How does Algernon's condition represent Charlie's condition?

REVIEW & RESOURCES

QUIZ

1. Who asks Charlie to keep his progress reports?

    A. Dr. Strauss
    B. Professor Nemur
    C. Burt Selden
    D. Alice Kinnian

2. How old is Charlie at the start of the novel?

    A. 32
    B. 36
    C. 26
    D. 6

3. Why does Alice recommend Charlie for the experiment?

    A. He is the smartest in his class
    B. He is friendly and will not give the scientists trouble
    C. The other students in her class refuse to take part in the experiment
    D. He is eager to learn

4. Who supervises Algernon's testing?

    A. Dr. Strauss
    B. Professor Nemur
    C. Burt
    D. Alice

5. In which progress report do Charlie's punctuation, spelling, and grammar improve most significantly?

    A. Progress Report 6
    B. Progress Report 7
    C. Progress Report 8
    D. Progress Report 9

6. Where is the scientists' convention held?

   A. New Orleans
   B. Chicago
   C. Boston
   D. San Francisco

7. Where is the Center for Retarded Adults where Charlie takes classes?

   A. The Welberg Foundation
   B. Columbia University
   C. Beekman College
   D. New York University

8. What is the first *hard* book that Charlie reads?

   A. *Paradise Lost*
   B. *The Wizard of Oz*
   C. *Robinson Crusoe*
   D. *The Wind in the Willows*

9. What does Charlie do when he learns that Gimpy has been stealing from Mr. Donner?

   A. He tells Gimpy that he will inform Mr. Donner unless Gimpy stops stealing
   B. He tells Mr. Donner that Gimpy has been stealing from him
   C. He steals the money back from Gimpy and returns it to the cash register without telling anyone
   D. He decides it is not his place to get involved

10. Which two characters suggest to Charlie that increasing his intelligence may be against God's will?

    A. Nemur and Strauss
    B. Alice and Fay
    C. Hilda and Fanny
    D. Gimpy and Rose

11. What job does Charlie's father have when Charlie finds him?

  A. Butcher
  B. Barber
  C. Salesman
  D. Night watchman

12. What book does Charlie tear apart near the end of the novel?

  A. *The Hindu Journal of Psychopathology*
  B. *The Algernon-Gordon Effect*
  C. *Paradise Lost*
  D. *Robinson Crusoe*

13. Which of the following is a reason that Fay proposes for Charlie's inability to make love to her?

  A. He is physically impotent
  B. He is a homosexual
  C. He does not know what sex is
  D. He is married

14. What is the range of Charlie's IQ in the novel?

  A. 70–110
  B. 72–140
  C. 65–160
  D. 68–185

15. Who threatens Charlie with a knife?

  A. Norma
  B. Nemur
  C. Gimpy
  D. Rose

16. Who does Charlie often hallucinate is watching him?

  A. His sister, Norma
  B. His mother, Rose
  C. A federal agent
  D. The "other" Charlie

REVIEW & RESOURCES

17. To whom does Charlie lose his virginity?

     A. Alice
     B. Fay
     C. A prostitute in Chicago
     D. A woman he meets in Central Park

18. What is the name of the companion mouse that Fay buys
     for Algernon?

     A. Fay Jr.
     B. Alger Hiss
     C. Minnie
     D. Moskowitz

19. What is the name of the quack doctor to whom Rose takes
     the six-year-old Charlie?

     A. Dr. Warren
     B. Dr. Guarino
     C. Dr. Acula
     D. Dr. Strauss

20. What name does Charlie give to his scientific theorem?

     A. The Gordon-Nemur Transfer
     B. The Algernon-Charlie Conundrum
     C. The Man-Mouse Prospectus
     D. The Algernon-Gordon Effect

21. What language is Charlie outraged to learn that Professor
     Nemur does not speak?

     A. German
     B. Hindi
     C. Latin
     D. Chinese

22. Of what does Nemur accuse Charlie during their argument after the cocktail party?

    A. Becoming arrogant and self-centered
    B. Stealing Burt's research
    C. Insulting Mrs. Nemur
    D. Not being as smart as he thinks he is

23. What does Alice tell Charlie she will do when he has reverted to his original IQ?

    A. Visit him every week
    B. Write to him every day
    C. Remain true to his memory
    D. Do her best to forget him

24. Where does Charlie go to live at the end of the novel?

    A. The Welberg Foundation
    B. With Norma
    C. The laboratory
    D. The Warren State Home

25. In what month does Charlie die?

    A. August
    B. September
    C. November
    D. Charlie does not die in the course of the novel

REVIEW & RESOURCES

SUGGESTIONS FOR FURTHER READING

KEYES, DANIEL. *Algernon, Charlie, and I: A Writer's Journey.* Boca Raton, Florida: Challcrest Press Books, 2000. (Contains the short-story version of "Flowers for Algernon," originally published in the April 4, 1959, issue of *The Magazine of Fantasy and Science Fiction.*)

SMALL, ROBERT, JR. "*Flowers for Algernon* by Daniel Keyes." In *Censored Books: Critical Viewpoints,* edited by Nicholas J. Karolides, Lee Burress, and John M. Kean, 249–255. Metuchen, New Jersey: Scarecrow, 1993.

SPARKNOTES
TEST PREPARATION
GUIDES

The SparkNotes team figured it was time to cut standardized tests down to size. We've studied the tests for you, so that SparkNotes test prep guides are:

Smarter:
Packed with critical-thinking skills and test-
taking strategies that will improve your score.

Better:
Fully up to date, covering all new features of the tests,
with study tips on every type of question.

Faster:
Our books cover exactly what you need to
know for the test. No more, no less.

SparkNotes Guide to the SAT & PSAT
SparkNotes Guide to the SAT & PSAT—Deluxe Internet Edition
SparkNotes Guide to the ACT
SparkNotes Guide to the ACT—Deluxe Internet Edition
SparkNotes Guide to the SAT II Writing
SparkNotes Guide to the SAT II U.S. History
SparkNotes Guide to the SAT II Math Ic
SparkNotes Guide to the SAT II Math IIc
SparkNotes Guide to the SAT II Biology
SparkNotes Guide to the SAT II Physics

SPARKNOTES STUDY GUIDES: